Astrology

Thorsons First Directions

Astrology
Charles and Suzi Harvey

To all who would hear the music of the spheres

Thorsons
An Imprint of HarperCollins*Publishers*
77-85 Fulham Palace Road,
Hammersmith, London W6 8JB

The Thorsons website address is:
www.thorsons.com

Published by Thorsons 2000

Text derived from *Principles of Astrology*, published by Thorsons, 1999

10 9 8 7 6 5 4 3 2 1

Editor: Jo Kyle
Design: Wheelhouse Creative Ltd.
Photography by PhotoDisc Europe Ltd.

A catalogue record for this book is available from the British Library

ISBN 0 0071 0332 8

Printed and bound in Hong Kong.

Contents

What is Astrology? 2

The History of Astrology 10

What can Astrology do for Me? 16

The Essential Elements of the Birth Chart 22

Putting It All Together 84

Resource Guide 88

Astrology

is the art and science of determining the potential of a person or nation by studying the position of the planets in the heavens relative to the earth below

'As above, so below'

What is Astrology?

Astrology is like a seed

Behind the light-hearted horoscopes of the newspapers lies a hidden wisdom that can help us understand more about ourselves and our lives. Astrology shows that each moment, such as that of our own birth, is like a seed, and within that seed is a blueprint that contains all our unlimited potential.

If this is your first astrology book, make a note of the time, date and place you obtained it. As you progress in your study you can look back at a map of this moment and see how it relates to the rest of your birth chart.

Getting a sense of the plot

To understand how astrology works it is useful to think about the whole process of creation. Whenever we make something, that thing is always the last thing to be manifested. For example, when we are preparing a meal we create a great deal of apparent chaos as raw materials are peeled, chopped, mixed with herbs, and so on. Creation is messy, and we have to keep our mind's eye focused on what we want the final creation to be if all the parts are to come together in the right way.

Similarly, our personal lives can seem very chaotic if we cannot see the underlying plot. This is where astrology can

help – by providing a sense of the plot. The birth chart has been called a kind of 'contract with time and space', and referring to this contract to remind ourselves of the overall game plan can help us to turn chaos into intelligence.

Through studying the birth chart, we find that what feels like chaos is often just an overemphasis or imbalance in certain areas – for example, too much water will make us too emotional, too little earth will mean we're not practical enough, an angular Mars will put us into overdrive, charging ahead at full-steam. Once we recognise this we are in a position to make more intelligent and informed life choices.

Astrology is an algebra, a symbolic language that helps us to read the contract, understand the plot, and imaginatively view the unique overall picture that is our life.

Astrology through time and space

Time and space define our lives. It is the cycles of time, such as the shift each day from dark to light, and the changing of the seasons, which rule the ebb and flow of daily life. At the particular time and place of your birth the planets, sun and moon were in a completely unique position in the sky. No other person will ever share exactly the same birthchart as you, not even an identical twin.

Astrology's perennial questions are:
When and where were you born?
When and where did this happen?

The planets and the signs of the zodiac

Astrology's vocabulary consists of the signs of the Zodiac, the planets and their aspects. Astrologers believe that each planet has distinct attributes and needs. Every birthchart contains all the planets, although the particular way they appear in each chart is what makes us unique.

   To early man the planets were 'wandering stars', following a distinct path through the heavens as they travel around the sun. The path they take was studied by early astrologers who mapped out its distinct stages and called it the cycle of the zodiac, or literally the 'circle of the animals', from the Greek zoon, as in a zoo. Each cycle was divided into 12 distinct phases, and each was given a distinct sign, usually an animal symbol.

   Each of the 12 signs represents a 30-degree arc in the sky, as seen from the Earth. As the Earth travels around the Sun it appears to pass from one arc to the next, going through all 12 arcs in one year. Someone born on 11th April has their birthday when the Sun passes through the arc called Aries, so this is their Sun Sign. Someone born on 11th May will have Taurus for their Sun sign.

Planetary cycles become days, weeks, months and years

Even if you are not aware of it, you are already familiar with some of the principles of astrology. The seven days of the week, which form the foundation of the way the world organizes its time, are named after the seven planets known to the ancient world. In fact, all the time frames we normally use are related to planetary cycles:

- a day is the time it takes for the Earth to rotate on its axis
- a week is a quarter of a lunar cycle
- a month is the time from one New Moon to the next
- a year is the time it takes for the Earth to go around the Sun

Astrology, potential and predestination

The birth chart may appear to be a 'static thing', something that will stay the same throughout your lifetime, but the way the planets continually move around the sun unfolds the chart's potential.

The planets complete their journey around the zodiac in different times. Jupiter's cycle, which influences our search for meaning, is about 12 years long. Saturn's takes about 29 years to complete, and the Saturn Return is a time of growing up and taking responsibility. The second Saturn Return, when we are 58, is when we examine what our life has achieved and start to face the inevitability of death. The Uranus cycle takes 84 years. During the half-way point of this planet's journey, at the age of about 40–42, people have their mid-life crisis.

Astrology is often thought to encourage a sense of predestination. People are sometimes apprehensive, frightened of learning the fate that awaits them. But we all have the power to shape our fate by changing our behaviour. So if we are exposed to either friendly or destructive forces we can use the knowledge we gain from astrology to try and achieve the best possible outcome in any given situation.

The History of Astrology

Who studies astrology?

Some of the greatest minds and most creative individuals through the centuries have studied astrology and found it to be a source of deep fascination, inspiration and guidance.

Some of the great literary giants of the past and of this century have also drawn insight, imagery and inspiration from astrology.

Pythagoras, Plato, St Thomas Aquinas, Galileo, Goethe, Ralph Waldo Emerson, W.B. Yeats and Jung all used astrology.

It still continues to enthral the minds of some of our finest contemporary thinkers, and to be used, behind the scenes, by some of the world's leading figures.

It is now well known that President Ronald Reagan never took any major initiative without optimizing the chances of success by getting the timing right. From his first inauguration as Governor of California to his declarations for the US Presidency, none of the major decisions in his life were taken without astrological advice.

Astrology past

The earliest records of most cultures and civilizations reveal that their world-view was based on astrology. Our oldest ancestors would have watched the cycles of day and night, the waxing and waning of the moon and the movements of the planets across the star-studded sky. Astrology appears to have emerged independently in different cultures around the world, and each seems to have had the same basic ideas about the relationship between above and below. All major ancient buildings, such as the Egyptian and Mayan Pyramids and Stonehenge appear to have been built so that they were aligned to the heavens above.

The significance of individual planets and stars is also very similar in different traditions. For example, Mars is always associated with fire, anger and war, whilst Venus is seen to be an essentially beneficent creature of beauty.

Astrology is central to the Jewish and Christian tradition. The Three Wise Men of the Bible who 'followed the star' were astrologers, and the particular 'star' they were following was almost certainly the dramatic coming together of the planets Jupiter and Saturn in Pisces, the sign of the fishes. And the symbol of the fish appears everywhere in early Christianity, such as Christ's designation, the 'fisher of men'.

Pythagoras, who lived in Greece around 600–540 BCE, was the first to put together a model of the astrological universe, and this was used around the world until the 17th century, when astrology was eclipsed by scientific discoveries. Astrology only re-emerged as a subject for popular study in the late 19th century, mainly through the passion of a few unconventional individuals.

Astrology present

Throughout the 20th century the work of a few dedicated individuals and organizations has helped astrology to develop into its present sophisticated form. The most important of these is the French psychologist Dr Michel Gauquelin and his wife Françoise, who in the 1950s made a study of thousands of birth certificates of famous people from all over Europe. They showed that successful professionals were usually born when particular planets were in particular positions.

- Future champion athletes, eminent military men and entrepreneurs tend to be born when Mars, god of the warrior, is at a specific angle.
- By contrast, future eminent scientists were born when Saturn, giver of a cautious, methodical, intellectual temperament, was prominent.
- Future actors and politicians had self-important, jovial Jupiter in these positions.
- Future politicians generally have an angular Moon, as do future writers and journalists.

During the 20th century, astrology has been gradually emerging from 200 years of isolation. It is still not accepted by most academics, and sociologists try to explain its enormous popular appeal as a superstitious reaction to the nihilism of the 20th century. Meanwhile, astrologers simply get on with their work, developing the study in exciting and challenging new areas.

Astrology was actually illegal in Britain until 1981 when the Vagrancy Act was repealed.

What can Astrology do for Me?

Astrology is best known for its power to describe character and its ability to 'look into the future'. However, the basic principles of astrology can be applied to almost every area of life.

Consulting an astrologer – what to expect

The information required by all astrologers is the date, time and place of birth. The time of your birth is crucial.

A typical first consultation will last between 90 minutes and two hours. Before you arrive, the astrologer will probably spend at least an hour preparing your natal chart, usually with the help of a computer, looking at current trends and making notes. When it is not possible to meet in person, some astrologers work very effectively by phone. Some will also supply a reading dictated on to a cassette.

Character analysis

Most practitioners' work will give you a character analysis. They will interpret your horoscope to build a personality profile of your talents, strengths and weaknesses. The consultation will reveal valuable insights about your personality and the dilemmas you experience in life, but it cannot change deep-seated behaviour patterns or heal wounds overnight.

If you find that the language of astrology really 'speaks' to you, it can become a path to help you make the life changes you desire. Most astrologers now undergo training to help them listen effectively and deal with the emotional responses of clients, rather than just giving them information.

Forecasting the future

Most of us want to know what will happen to us in the future. Astrology can never answer these questions in absolute terms. The astrologer looking at a chart cannot see 'events' and people written on it. However, they can see combinations of energy and patterns of ideas which are likely to manifest in certain ways.

  By studying the chart it is possible to see the kinds of issues that are likely to arise in a person's life. Knowing the kind of energies that will be to the fore at a particular time, the astrologer will suggest ways in which they can be most constructively directed.

  Likewise, astrology cannot 'foretell the future' as such, although it can look at the qualities of a particular period and, like a weather forecaster, make intelligent guesses about the kind of issues you are likely to be facing.

Relationships

There is a whole branch of astrology devoted to the study of the way people are likely to get on with each other. By comparing different birth charts, an astrologer can give you insights about the kind of people you may get on with and the dynamics that will emerge in the relationship.

This type of comparison will be much deeper than just looking at your Sun signs. While different Sun signs are more or less compatible with one another, the comparison of charts is much more complex.

Different astrological types will have different kinds of relationships and astrology can be used to understand the kinds of things we want in a relationship and the issues that will be important for us.

Careers

Astrology can be invaluable in helping you find a rewarding career. The birth chart cannot say that someone will be a musician or social worker or accountant. However, it can indicate that, for example, music, or the care of others, or the effective and creative handling of resources, are things you will probably enjoy and at which you have a good chance of personal satisfaction and success.

Choosing the best time

If you launch a boat it is simpler to wait for the tide to come in and float the boat off the shore than to push it down the beach and across the shingle. Choosing the right time to start any particular project has always been a major role for the astrologer. In business, the time to start a project will depend both on the nature of the work and the chart of the people closely involved with it. For example, if you are arranging a mail-out and want to make sure you have the best chance of your communication being read, it is a good idea to ensure that Mercury, planet of communication, and the Moon, which rules the mood of the moment, are well placed.

Getting married

Getting married is a major venture for anyone, and if you have a choice, it makes good sense to plan the timing. This can optimize the chances of a long-lasting and happy bond. Indeed, throughout the Indian sub-continent and much of Asia, few couples will get married without first ensuring that the day is a propitious one for them. Here the astrologer will look at the possible dates and see which dates and times yield the most harmonious charts; and they will also consider the relationship between this chart and the charts of both bride and groom.

The late poet laureate, Ted Hughes, was very interested in astrology, and describes the astrological factors surrounding his meeting with Sylvia Plath in the award-winning poem Birthday Letters.

'That day the solar system married us
 Whether we knew it or not.'

The Essential Elements of the Birth Chart

So how does an astrologer find out all this information? When they study a horoscope, they are looking at a unique combination of four essential parts:

- The planets (*see page* 23) represent our psychological urges or functions, our different kinds of energies and needs.
- The signs (*see page* 54) show the way in which a planet's energy will express itself.
- The houses (*see page* 80) locate the action in specific areas of life, such as home, career and relationships.

- The aspects (*see page* 44) bring in the planetary relationships, and how they influence the talents, strengths, weaknesses, conflicts and aspirations of the individual.

The planets

Astrology is built on the idea that the solar system is a whole, with each part of that system affecting each other part. And the planets play a crucial part within this system. Therefore, in human beings astrologers believe the planets represent parts or functions of the whole personality, each having its own essential energy and purpose, each forming a different 'side' of us. Every birth chart features all ten astrological planets, each in a different position and each playing a different part.

The Sun

The Sun is our nearest star, a luminous ball of fire that is the source of almost all the solar system's heat, light and energy. The Sun represents the life-force, it gives individuality and self-expression. The Sun is associated with kingship, authority and creative power.

   The Sun gives us purpose and helps us develop confident self-expression. When we are in touch with our Sun we enjoy life creatively, when we're not we can end up feeling distanced and depressed.

- People with very strong Suns have a commanding presence; they're in the world to be noticed and to be appreciated.
- Too much Sun in their chart can make them arrogant, vain and tyrannical.
- A typical Sun type is Madonna who is a flashy Sun Leo.
- In the body: the Sun rules the heart.
- In the zodiac: The sun rules fiery Leo.
- In your chart: the Sun is the core of individuality, the inner guiding light.

The Moon

The Moon circles the Earth every month, marking out the ebb and flow of daily life and causing the tidal motions of the seas. The Moon represents the transitional nature of life, the way that one phase organically gives rise to the next.

   The Moon symbolizes the flowing, receptive, feminine aspect of life. It is our impulse to protect and nurture. While we need the Sun to be focused and make conscious decisions, the Moon is central to our unconscious life and imagination.

- The Moon is the 'inner' you, with moods and private feelings.
- An over-emphasis of lunar influence makes you irrational, moody and clingy.
- A typical Moon type is Susan Sarandon, the hugely empathic acctress who has portrayed the entire female spectrum (Moon exactly rising).
- In the body: The Moon rules fertility, bodily fluids and digestion.
- In the Zodiac: The Moon rules Cancer.
- In your chart: The Moon is our feeling life and need for others.

Mercury

Mercury is the swift-moving planet closest to the Sun. It represents mental activity: language, communication, interpretation, the ability to gather facts and to see relationships between things. Mercury allows us to put information together to make sense of ourselves in the world.

   Through Mercury we experience curiosity and apply our minds to learning and communicating. Mercury is especially active in the market place and in politics and theatre, where swiftness and brilliance of intellectual argument can win any debate.

- Mercurial individuals are quick thinkers and fast talkers, often extremely intelligent and learned, and usually wiry and restless with a sensitive nervous system.
- An excess of Mercury may mean you waste energy through too much talking and thinking.
- A typical Mercurial figure is the clever and swift-moving Puck in *A Midsummer Night's Dream*.
- In the body: Mercury is associated with the five senses, through which we gain knowledge of our world, and the nervous system, which sends messages between the brain and other parts of the body.
- In the Zodiac: Mercury rules Gemini and Virgo.
- In your chart: Mercury shows the characteristic way you think and talk.

Venus

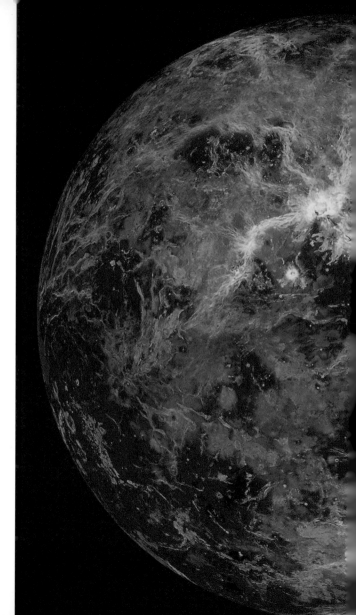

Venus is the goddess of love and beauty. She represents our need to relate, our desire for love and affection, and our appreciation of beauty. Venus is connected with what we value most, whether that be ideals, relationships, works of art or money. Venus rules both Taurus and Libra.

Through Taurus we see her lusty, sensual side and, if we remember how hot and steamy it is on Venus, we get a sense of the sexual passions that the goddess can arouse. Through Libra she expresses her beauty in a more idealized and civilized way. This side desires loving connections with others through social encounters, teamwork, fair play and harmony. Venus represents the part of us that easily attracts what we want, rather than going out in 'hot pursuit' (a job for Mars). Venus is a 'lucky' energy, bringing us the nice things in life.

- Strongly Venusian individuals are sociable and friendly, love pleasurable social pursuits and artistic environments, and need others to feel balanced and completed.
- Too much Venus can result in over-indulgence, superficiality and promiscuity.
- A classic Venus type is the glamorous, seductive actress Marilyn Monroe (Venus conjunct the Midheaven).
- In the body: Venus rules the kidneys.
- In the zodiac: Venus rules Taurus and Libra.
- In your chart: Venus represents the way you express affection and your aesthetic and social values.

Mars

Mars, the god of War, represents our instinct for survival. Mars brings us the bravery to defend our territory and is expressed through the sex drive, ensuring the survival of the species. Through Mars we say 'no' or 'yes' and then initiate action; we claim our 'rights' and defend our personal worth.

When we are thwarted, Mars is our anger. Mars wants to win. But Mars is not just the instinct of self-assertion and competition; we need Mars in order to 'do' anything. A deficiency of Mars produces the 'door mat' personality, someone who cannot defend themselves.

- Strongly Martial individuals are go-getters, people who love a challenge and are unafraid of vigorous, even dangerous, confrontation.
- An excess of Mars makes one contentious, quarrelsome, over-aggressive and violent.
- A typical Mars type is the champion tennis player John McEnroe (Sun square Mars) who also displays an excess of Mars (Mars opposed Jupiter and square Pluto) in his temper.
- In the body: Mars expresses itself through the sex drive, the muscles, the red blood cells and adrenaline.
- In the zodiac: Mars rules Aries and Scorpio.
- In your sign: Mars shows how self-assertive you are and how great your drive to succeed.

Jupiter

Jupiter is a powerful law-giver, supremely masculine and creative, representing opportunity and growth. Jupiter – or 'Jove' – gives us the words jovial, joy and jubilation, and Jupiterian individuals are usually bursting with new ideas and positive feelings. Due to the positive outlook they bring to life, luck is seen to be with them more than any other planetary type.

Jupiter gives us the urge to expand and to explore beyond our familiar culture. It inspires us to find the truth, to pursue intellectual meaning and a greater understanding. An excess of Jupiter can create over-indulgence, arrogance and a tendency to 'play God', to feel that we are above the law. Jupiter's excesses may also lead to waste.

- Strongly Jupiterian individuals are the leaders in society; they may be generous philanthropists or flashy movie stars whose personal dramas are projected out onto the world screen for all to see.
- Too much Jupiter makes us 'big-headed' and 'too big for our boots'.
- A typical Jupiter type is the colourful politician and successful fiction writer Jeffrey Archer (Sun conjunct Jupiter).
- In the body: Jupiter is associated with the liver and the metabolism of fats and sugar, so Jupiter's excesses are quickly evident when they become unhealthy for us.
- In the zodiac: Jupiter rules fiery Sagittarius and is the co-ruler of Pisces.
- In your chart: Jupiter shows the way in which we seek to expand and make the most of our opportunities.

Saturn

Saturn is Father Time, the ancient ruler of fate, limits, responsibilities and structure. Traditionally depicted with a scythe and known as the Grim Reaper, Saturn has always inspired dread and fear, for he is the god who brings obstacles, trials, pain, loneliness and endings.

However, by surviving and learning from such trials, we become stronger and can carve out a real identity. Saturn's purpose is to help us learn endurance, determination and discipline in order to achieve our dreams.

- Saturnine individuals are serious, conservative and self-controlled; self-reliant, dependable, resourceful and wise. They usually feel a need to make a useful contribution to society.
- Saturn's negative qualities can be emotional repression, fear and an unwillingness to accept anything fresh and innovative.
- A typical Saturn type is the Conservative Prime Minister Margaret Thatcher (Saturn exactly rising) who emphasized the need for every individual to assume personal responsibility.
- In the body: Saturn gives structure and support through the skeletal system, as well as boundaries and definition through the skin.
- In the zodiac: Saturn rules ambitious, earthy Capricorn, and also co-rules Aquarius, a sign associated with analysis and the search for truth.
- In your chart: Saturn reveals how you will experience authority, accept responsibility and deal with obstacles in your life.

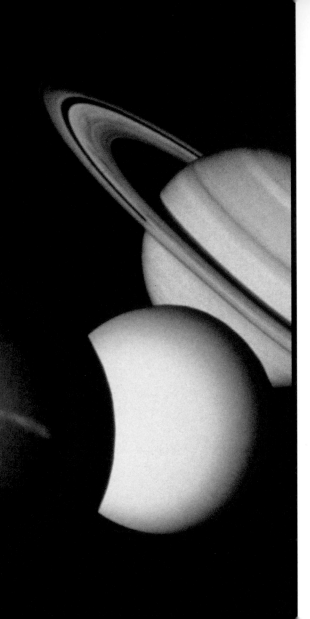

Uranus

Uranus was discovered in 1781 as the world was entering its most radical phase, with revolutions erupting in Europe and the newly colonized America. A spirit of rebellion was born and Uranus is the energy that rejects the limits of the status quo for individuality and independence.

Uranians constantly look for new breakthroughs and new freedoms. They are the risk-takers with the courage to shock society with radically different views; the visionaries who take society towards a brave new world.

- Strongly Uranian individuals are often seen as eccentric outsiders who bring a message society needs to hear, they remind society that everybody has a 'mad' – or acutely original – side which needs acceptance.
- Those with too much Uranus are anarchic and inflexible, and can pay dearly for their boldness by being rejected by society.
- A typical Uranus type is Sigmund Freud (Sun conjunct Uranus) whose genius opened up the whole new frontier of man's inner mind.
- In the body: Uranus is associated with the nervous system.
- In the zodiac: Uranus rules Aquarius, a sign whose viewpoint is often challenging and prophetic.
- In your chart: Uranus reveals the way in which you express your originality.

Neptune

Neptune, the God of the sea, rules the watery depths. Its discovery in
1846 came at a time of many Neptunian developments, such as the
invention of steam power for travel, the use of anaesthetics for pain
relief and the increase of a social conscience which brought homes for
the poor.

   Neptune represents our urge to merge, to experience blissful union
with another. Falling in love is a kind of Neptunian romantic 'spell'

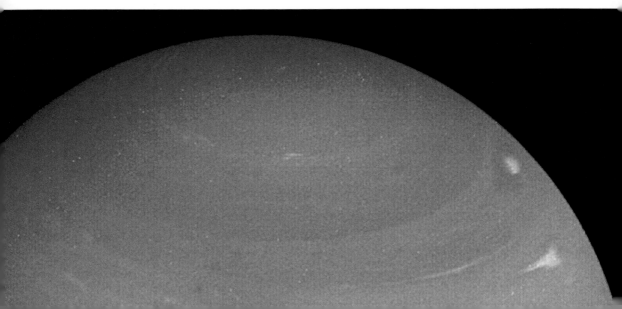

where we long to belong utterly to the beloved. The goal of all religions is essentially a Neptunian one: union with the Divine. Neptune is associated with fantasy and myth, dreams and visions, magic and beauty that transcends everyday limits.

- Neptune brings us the potential for inspired artistic creativity and is strong in the charts of artists, actors and musicians, as well as highly gifted healers and therapists.
- Too much Neptune can make us gullible, emotionally fragile and prone to delusions.
- A typical Neptune type is the inspired composer Mozart (Sun opposed Neptune).
- In the body: Neptune rules the lymphatic system which recognizes and destroys foreign entities.
- In the zodiac: Neptune rules watery, enigmatic and versatile Pisces.
- In your chart: Neptune reveals the way you express your imagination and your desire for romantic and spiritual union.

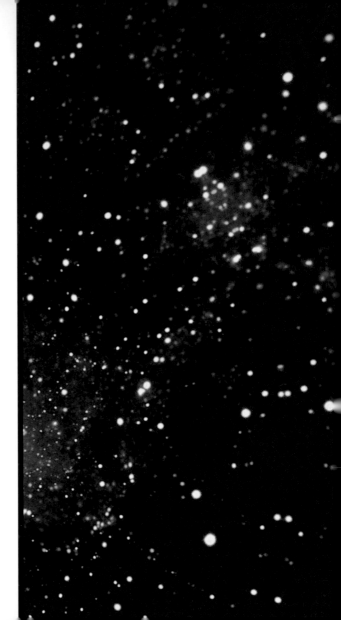

Pluto

Pluto is both creator and destroyer. It is a powerful elemental force that works away below the surface and periodically erupts into conscious awareness. This last planet in our solar system was discovered in 1930, a time that ushered in the use of atomic power, a discovery that marked a pivotal point of no return in mankind's history: will we use this power creatively or destructively? This time also saw the rise of fascism, and a more widespread acceptance of psychoanalysis.

Pluto rules the fundamental transformational processes of life – birth, sex and death. Pluto's energy brings intense upheaval and transformation and can be seen in natural disasters, the birth process, or a psychological breakdown or breakthrough.

- Plutonians are attracted to mysteries and want to get to the bottom of things; they are often found in police work, scientific and medical research, paranormal studies and psychoanalytical work where an essential quality is the courage to face pain and difficult truths.
- Too much Plutonian influence can make us suspicious, controlling and power-hungry.
- A typical Pluto type is the revolutionary Chinese leader, Mao Tse Tung (Sun/Moon = Pluto).
- In the body: Pluto rules the processes of elimination and regeneration at every level.
- In the zodiac: Pluto rules Scorpio, the sign of passionate desire and penetrating insight.
- In your chart: Pluto shows how you experience your basic urges and the tension between stasis and change.

The aspects

What are the planets in your chart saying to each other?

The next major factor in your birth chart is the aspects. While planets can, and do at times, exert their influence completely independently, it is fascinating to study the way they interplay with the other planets.

To understand what an aspect is, we need to remember that, over time, each planet moves through a cycle of 360 degrees with each other planet. We all know this cycle from the monthly phases of the Moon, where it moves around the Earth and forms different aspects with the Sun, in cycles of about 28 days. Planets can be seen together in the sky and then gradually separating as they move through a 360-degree relationship with one another. At each phase of this cycle their relationship will be different. If two planets are close together – which astrologers call 'in conjunction' – they will be obliged to talk and work with one another. If they stand on opposite sides of the circle they will be 'in opposition' and tend to oppose and contradict one another.

These changing positions come about because the planets move at very different speeds. Mercury, which is the closest planet to the Sun, takes just 88 days to complete one orbit, whilst Pluto, the most distant, takes some 246 years. Because of this difference in speed, a faster planet can be seen to catch up with a slower planet, join it for a moment, the moment of 'conjunction', and then move on ahead. In due course, the faster planet arrives at a point in its orbit at which it is opposite the slower planet, this is when it is in 'opposition'. It then moves on round to the next conjunction. The aspects mark out the different main stages of this cycle.

The aspect grid

To discover which planets are on talking terms in your chart, the astrologer calculates an 'aspect grid', which will show which planets are 'in aspect' or 'in a harmonic relationship' with each other. If you visit an astrologer and have your chart drawn up, the significant aspects will give the reading much more depth and individuality.

Aspects are like relationships

Aspects, like relationships, come in many varieties. Some are simple and straightforward; others are subtler and more complex. For example, Venus and Jupiter both like the good things in life, and will make a happy union. But Venus and Saturn in conjunction is more of a marriage of opposites and makes for harder work. So, too, the house (*see page* 80) a planet occupies will have its impact on the quality of the relationship. Often, many of the planets are aspected together, and this will create further fascinating combinations and psychological complexity.

The four elements

Along with the planets and their aspects, the most important elements of the birth chart are the signs of the zodiac. And in the circle of the zodiac there are four elements – Fire, Earth, Air and Water – and three ways these are expressed – Cardinal, Fixed and Mutable.

- **Cardinal energy** has an initiating quality; when the Sun enters the Cardinal signs (Aries, Cancer, Libra, Capricorn) a new season begins.

- **Fixed energy** has a consolidating quality; each season comes to its fullest expression when the Sun travels through these signs (Taurus, Leo, Scorpio, Aquarius).

- **Mutable energy** has a circulating quality; as the Sun moves through these signs (Gemini, Virgo, Sagittarius, Pisces) we can feel that change is in the air and the seasons are making way for a new phase.

Each of us has all the elements within us, although we feel most confident using only one or two of them most of the time.

The planets feel more or less at home in different elements. These elements appear in an orderly sequence around the zodiac, starting with the fire sign Aries and repeating the pattern Fire, Earth, Air, Water, three times.

Fire *Aries, Leo, Sagittarius*

Fire is a masculine, positive element, bringing light and transformation. Fire is unpredictable, unstable, but it can also be warming, exciting and creative.

- **Strengths:** Fiery temperaments are positive and extrovert, pushing ahead in life with charismatic confidence. They are demonstrative, dramatic and intense, with a strong intuitive side.
- **Weaknesses:** Fire individuals can 'get burned' by their excessive enthusiasm and impulsiveness, and may feel depression when brought up short.

- **Aries** – Cardinal Fire – is impulsive and pioneering; spontaneous, outspoken, headstrong.
- **Leo** – Fixed Fire – is more stable, regal and kingly; happy in situations where power and responsibility must be handled wisely.
- **Sagittarius** – Mutable Fire – fires sparks in all directions on its endless search for meaning and self-discovery.

Earth *Taurus, Virgo, Capricorn*

Earth is solid, where we live and work and make all our exciting visions become reality. No matter what our fantasies and wishes are, we must stay 'grounded' in reality to make them happen.

- **Strengths:** The earthy individual is practical, sensible, conservative, dependable and capable of running a business or household efficiently.
- **Weaknesses:** If an earthy individual lacks Fire, their lack of vision may hold them back, and they can become narrow, sluggish and obstinate.

- **Taurus** – Fixed Earth – is sensual, determined and patient, but also very stubborn when its security is threatened.
- **Virgo** – Mutable Earth – will analyse and organize things into logical and efficient routines.
- **Capricorn** – Cardinal Earth – has a very ambitious, aspiring approach to life.

Air *Gemini, Libra, Aquarius*

Air, although not as unstable and assertive as Fire, is also an extrovert element, a thinking type who will always look for the rational way to do things.

- **Strengths:** Air excels at clear, objective reasoning and has a capacity for lively communication. Airy temperaments are gregarious but civilized, curious but co-operative, intellectual but casual and often witty, fun-loving and sociable.
- **Weaknesses:** Can be uncomfortable with feelings or overly intellectual.

- **Gemini** – Mutable Air – loves to experience a variety of people and experiences.
- **Libra** – Cardinal Air – seeks justice, harmony and co-operation.
- **Aquarius** – Fixed Air – is interested in ideas and devoted to the common good.

Water *Cancer, Scorpio, Pisces*

Water is the most mysterious element. It is cooling, refreshing and nurturing; it can also be mysterious and forbidding or overwhelming and engulfing. Water symbolises empathy and feeling and our need to connect emotionally with others.

- **Strengths:** Sympathetic, romantic, intuitive, psychic and sensitive.
- **Weaknesses:** Can be subject to mysterious, unfathomable moods and secretiveness.

- **Cancer** – Cardinal Water – is cautious, caring and artistic.
- **Scorpio** – Fixed Water – is passionate, possessive and unafraid of facing the darker human emotions.
- **Pisces** – Mutable Water – is highly imaginative, chameleon-like, and compassionate.

The signs of the zodiac

Like the planets, the signs of the zodiac play a central role in Astrology.

The circle of the zodiac traces the path of the Earth's journey around the Sun. Each sign of the zodiac symbolizes a vital phase of life, as well as a basic personality type.

The zodiac was first described by early astrologers who watched the path of the planets around the sky and called it the cycle of the zodiac, literally the 'circle of the animals'. Each cycle was divided into 12 distinct phases, and each was given a distinct sign.

Aries **Positive • Cardinal • Fire**

The Sun passes through Aries between about 21 March–19 April

Aries is the first sign of the zodiac and has a thrusting, raw energy and an instinct for action and leadership. Ruled by Mars, the god of war and competition, Aries is daring, impulsive, enterprising, sometimes foolhardy, but always optimistic. Aries is represented by the ram.

  Bold, dynamic, assertive, the Aries individual, whether male or female, has a strong masculine creative drive. Aries is competitive, restless and independent; he needs to conquer, to feel that he can make a difference to his world. Aries loves to initiate and is not worried

about the mistakes that could be made through rash action.

Aries loves a difficult challenge and gets bored with too much self-reflection. Aries is always optimistic and has faith in his abilities to master problems. There is a naivety and vulnerability about Aries that is often hidden underneath a rough exterior. Aries is loyal and passionately devoted to family and loved ones, although he always needs freedom to pursue his own career and interests.

- If Aries is strong in your birth chart, you will spend much of your life defining your identity, learning how to assert your will, achieving recognition.
- Impatience and recklessness are Aries' downfall.
- A typical Arian is the poet Swinburne who wrote in 'The Hymn to Man': 'Glory to Man in the highest! For Man is the master of things.'
- Aries rules the head and its motto is 'I am'.

Taurus **Negative • Fixed • Earth**

The Sun passes through Taurus between about 20 April–20 May

Solid, nurturing and stabilizing, the bull is the symbol of Taurus, representing strength, passion and instinct. Ruled by Venus, the goddess of love and beauty, Taureans are easy-going, lovers of beauty and good food, in touch with the body and their basic needs. Taureans make good organizers, teachers, parents – anything that requires care, patience, diligence and down-to-earth common sense.

Taureans form deep attachments to their loved ones, home and possessions, and tend to distrust anything they cannot touch, taste or measure. They are famous for their extreme obstinacy and can literally dig in their heels when challenged.

- If Taurus is highly emphasized in your birth chart, you will try to build your identity through work and a solid material base, and enjoy the pleasures of the natural world.
- Taurean obstinacy makes them prone to getting stuck in a rut. They can also become possessive and materialistic, and their occasional over-indulgence can lead to weight problems.
- A typical Taurean is composer Irving Berlin whose most famous song sums up what Taureans love best: 'Doing what comes naturally'.
- Taurus rules the throat and neck, and its motto is 'I possess'.

Gemini   Positive • Mutable • Air

The Sun passes through Gemini between about 21 May–20 June

Gemini is the most versatile and changeable sign, and loves studying the complexities of people and of life. Gemini is ruled by Mercury, the ancient god of the intellect and swift communication, which makes for natural communicators, teachers, writers and go-betweens. Gemini often comes out with brilliant insights and witticisms, but like the restless butterfly, doesn't want to dwell on the details. In general, Gemini hates two things: boredom and emotional displays.

Geminian energy is notoriously asexual and amoral: it needs to be able to move and experiment. Geminians are playful, searching, sociable, perceptive and refreshing. This is the Peter Pan of the zodiac, forever resisting the commitment of adulthood and keeping all options open.

- If Gemini is strongly emphasized in your birth chart, you will always need variety and stimulation, and much of your life will focus on mental activities and verbal and written communication.
- Too much Gemini can make you irresponsible, reluctant to acknowledge your emotional needs and content to skim the surface of life.
- Actor John Barrymore expressed the typical Geminian duality: 'One of my chief regrets during my years in the theatre is that I couldn't sit in the audience and watch me.'
- Gemini rules the arms and hands, and its motto is 'I communicate'.

Cancer   Negative • Cardinal • Water

The Sun passes through Cancer between about 21 June–22 July

Cancer's symbol is the crab and it represents the emotional bonds that link us to our family, our past and also to the future. The crab is a creature of both sea and land, and Cancer will be drawn towards the watery, imaginative depths as well as the secure homes into which they scuttle when danger appears. The Cancerian's defences are like the crab's: a crusty exterior protects a vulnerable interior, and they will shift and move around a problem until they come up with a solution.

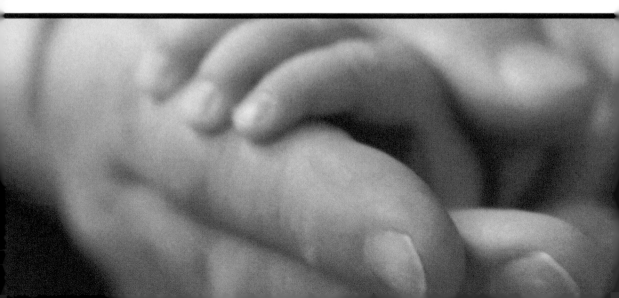

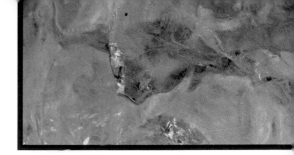

Ruled by the Moon, Cancerians are very emotional and their moods wax and wane. One minute they may be clear-headed, affectionate and helpful, the next dreamy or withdrawn. Cancerians need something to nurture and fuss over, like a mother hen. Cancerian characteristics include sensitivity, intuition, compassion, devotion, a deep urge to be needed and appreciated. But Cancer is not only poetic and imaginative; it is also a sign with a shrewd business sense.

- If Cancer is strongly emphasized in your birth chart, you will focus a lot of energy on trying to understand your emotions.
- Too much Cancer can make you subject to irrational moods and sulkiness
- Cancerian writer Anne Morrow Lindberg expressed this water sign's emotional yearning: 'I want first of all to be at peace with myself, I want to live an inner harmony, essentially spiritual.'
- Cancer rules the breast and the stomach, and its motto is 'I belong'.

Leo **Positive • Fixed • Fire**

The Sun passes through Leo between about 23 July–22 August

Leo is ruled by the Sun, the centre of our solar system, and its symbol is the lion, a noble and dangerous beast who is best not thwarted. Leo is concerned with individuality, the need for recognition and respect amidst a larger group. Rather like a child, the Leo personality always

wants to be the centre of attention and is acutely aware of its impact on others. Leo's energy is loyal, steadfast, and confident. Leo's intense idealism makes them fine leaders and organizers; and their love of drama means they are often drawn to work in the theatre.

- If you have Leo strongly emphasized in your chart, much of your life will focus on expressing the radiance of your unique self and gaining recognition from the outside world.
- Too much Leo can make you arrogant and tyrannical. Strongly Leonine personalities are extremely self-absorbed and can tend to think that the world revolves around them.
- Novelist Bernice Rubens expressed a typical Leo sentiment: 'The secret is to be true to yourself.'
- Leo rules the heart, and its motto is 'I create'.

Virgo Negative • Mutable • Earth

The Sun passes through Virgo between about 23 August–23 September

Virgo is ruled by Mercury, the god of intellect, and Virgo personalities always need to be usefully engaged. They will study hard to acquire the skills they need to lead a useful and productive life. Virgoan qualities include a desire to serve and to improve, versatility, good powers of analysis and critical thinking, self-doubt, modesty and self-sufficiency.

Virgo's deepest satisfaction comes from knowing he or she has done a job well. Virgos will work hard to improve themselves and this can make them very serious and self-critical: they aspire to perfection and this is often their Achilles heel. Being skilled at ordering and serving, Virgo is attracted to roles involving organization and practical analysis and their drive for perfection means they are often exceptionally fine craftsmen and artists.

- If Virgo is strongly emphasized in your chart, you will spend much of your life in some kind of service, on streamlining your talents, and mastering skills that bring greater efficiency and enjoyment at work.
- Virgo's perfectionism can make them irritable and cause them health problems and they often have to learn to let go and enjoy themselves.
- Leo Tolstoy was a typical Virgoan, who said: 'the vocation of every man and woman is to serve other people.'
- Virgo rules the digestive system and its motto is 'I perfect and serve'.

Libra **Positive • Cardinal • Air**

The Sun passes through Libra between about 24 September–23 October

Ruled by Venus, the planet of social harmony, love and beauty, Libra aspires to balance in all things and is very idealistic. Librans value equality and justice. Sweet-tempered and easy-going, but with a feistiness beneath the surface, Librans are often very good at managing people and getting the best out of them. They have a strong need to

relate to others which makes them more dependent than they appear. Being an air sign, Libra prefers to rationally observe and discuss things in a civilized manner, and their idealism may take them into law and politics.

Librans seek to communicate and may express their creative struggle through literature, theatre and art. They are always considered, civilized and co-operative.

- If Libra is strongly emphasized in your chart, you will invest a great deal of personal energy in friendships and relationships, and these will be both a challenge and a source of great nourishment.
- Trying to consider many different viewpoints can make Libra chronically indecisive.
- Oscar Wilde was a characteristic Libran: 'It is absurd to divide people into good and bad. People are either charming or tedious.'
- Libra rules the kidneys, and its motto is 'I balance'.

Scorpio Negative • Fixed • Water

The Sun passes through Scorpio between about 23 October–21 November

Scorpio's ancient ruler, Mars, symbolizes willpower and strength, something Scorpio has in abundance. Scorpio also has a secretive and regenerative side, and is known for his intense feelings. Scorpio's mascot is the scorpion, a nocturnal creature that attacks itself when cornered. This reflects Scorpio's instinct to retaliate, and also his ability to survive life's most dangerous and painful experiences.

Scorpio is intensely emotional; he grapples with the darker side of life in order to get to the truth, and has the courage and wisdom to confront it so he can ultimately use truth for healing and regeneration.

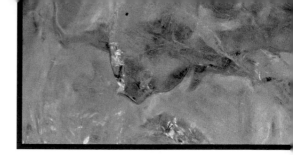

Scorpios often have a mysterious charisma. Equal to their self-protection is their extraordinary commitment and devotion to those they love. Their fascination with human nature and power often takes them into medicine, psychology and politics. As a water sign, Scorpio is painfully aware of human vulnerability.

- If Scorpio is strongly emphasized in your birth chart, you will seek to understand the intensities of human relationships and the complexities of the human appetite.
- Scorpio's intensity can be experienced by others as demanding and overwhelming and they can appear secretive, possessive, vengeful and manipulative.
- Classic Scorpio Bram Stoker, the author of Dracula, expressed typically Scorpion themes in his work: 'Ah, sir, you dwellers in the city cannot enter into the feelings of the hunter.'
- Scorpio rules the genitals and excretory system, and its motto is 'I regenerate'.

Sagittarius **Positive • Mutable • Fire**

The Sun passes through Sagittarius between about 22 November–21 December

The symbol for Sagittarius is the half-man, half-horse archer, clutching his bow and arrow and aiming towards some distant goal. Sagittarius is ruled by Jupiter, has a masculine creativity and active intellect and is full of aspirations. Sagittarius loves to travel, to learn and meet new cultures. Sagittarians are open and benevolent, genuinely interested in what makes people act and live in certain ways.

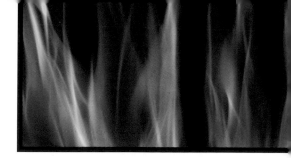

Sagittarian energy is warm, friendly and alert. They are restless, optimistic, and always trying to understand, enthusiastically searching for meaning. Independent, proud, boisterous, the Sagittarian always needs plenty of space, at work and in relationships. They will rebel against meaningless rules, but respect those with integrity and honesty.

- If Sagittarius is strongly emphasized in your chart, your life will be dominated by a desire for meaning beyond the boundaries of normal existence.
- Too much Sagittarian energy can make you pompous, careless and flighty. Your love for the large and dramatic means you sometimes promise too much and overstretch yourself.
- The Sagittarian author and satirist Mark Twain expressed this sign's restless, ironic mind when he wrote: 'Why shouldn't truth be stranger than fiction? Fiction, after all, has to make sense.'
- Sagittarius rules the thighs and its motto is 'I aspire'.

Capricorn Negative • Cardinal • Earth

The Sun passes through Capricorn between about 22 December–19 January

Capricorn's symbol is the upwardly mobile mountain goat and it is the most ambitious and determined of the Earth signs. Capricorn's ruling planet is Saturn, the symbol of authority, responsibility and tradition. The Capricornian personality is hard-working, cautious, serious and reserved, intent on understanding and constructively using their wisdom to build a secure future.

   Capricorn is not easily discouraged by difficult challenges, having very definite aims. They place great importance on proving their stamina and ability and such serious staying power often makes it hard

for them to relax and enjoy life. Early in life the Capricorn individual seems filled with adult concerns and responsibilities. But as they get older and more secure, Capricorn paradoxically grows younger and more playful. Dependable and loyal, Capricorns keep their promises and make excellent leaders. They are very concerned with order, duty and discipline, and prefer to hide their vulnerability.

- If Capricorn is strongly emphasized in your chart, you will spend much of your life defining and pursuing professional ambitions of which you can be proud.
- The weak Capricorn, driven by a powerful need for recognition, can build their empires on faulty foundations, and can find failure very hard to bear.
- Capricorn Stephen Hawking overcame great physical obstacles to pursue his pioneering work in astronomy. He wrote: 'The progress of the human race in understanding the universe has established a small corner of order in an increasingly disordered universe.'
- Capricorn rules the bones and skeletal system, and its motto is 'I order'.

Aquarius Positive • Fixed • Air

The Sun passes through Aquarius between about 20 January–18 February

Although its symbol is the Water-bearer Aquarius is an Air sign concerned with universal ideals. Aquarius is ruled by both Saturn and Uranus, and is interested in the laws that support society and protect the rights of the individual. As a personality, Aquarius is intellectual, unconventional, visionary, often scientific, independent and usually altruistic. These individuals have an anarchic streak and are interested in leaderless, egalitarian communities.

   Aquarians are drawn to new people with an openness and curiosity that is both liberating and at times exasperating – often Aquarius is

not aware of the subtleties of emotional relationships. Friendly and gregarious, Aquarius can also be naive and slightly eccentric. They challenge assumptions and wake people up. Although Aquarians are independent people who need a lot of space for self-expression, they are not without passion. It's just that they find it easier to express this in politics than in one-to-one relationships.

- If Aquarius is strongly emphasized in your chart, you will want to find a meaningful role in a social group, and you may risk being the outsider in order to contribute to the greater good.
- Too much Aquarius can make you rigid in your beliefs due to an unshakeable faith in ideals. It can also make you difficult to live with and a loner, more at home with your ideas than your feelings.
- Russian playwright Anton Chekov expressed typical Aquarian views: 'Man has been endowed with reason, with the power to create, so that he can add to what he's been given.'
- Aquarius rules the lower legs and the circulation, and its motto is 'I reform'.

Pisces   **Negative • Mutable • Water**

The Sun passes through Pisces between about 19 February–20 March

The symbol for Pisces is the two fishes, each swimming in a different direction, and Neptune, the god of the sea, rules Pisces. Jesus was known as 'the fisher of men', and his love and compassion gave him the power to sacrifice his earthly life for all humanity. Many Pisceans have a similar self-sacrificing, forgiving, compassionate nature and are capable of emotionally identifying with the plight of the suffering. But they can also sacrifice their fondest dreams due to indecisiveness and lack of confidence.

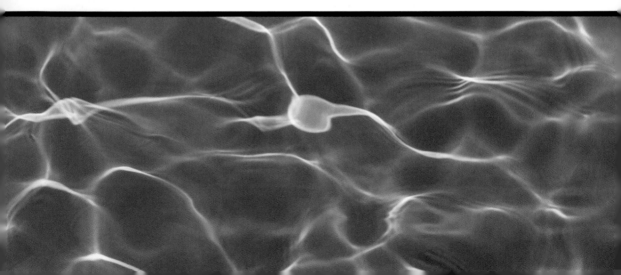

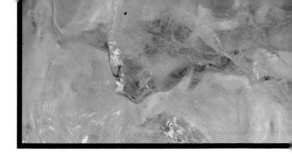

Although they have a sensual and sociable side, Pisceans also have a very private side where they hold their dreams and fantasies. This sign is very receptive to the emotional currents in others, intuitive and psychic. This openness means they can go either way: some are drawn to alcohol and drugs, others are gifted in the healing professions. The theatre is an ideal platform for Pisces; a place for them to move in and out of different identities easily.

- If Pisces is strongly emphasized in your chart, you will need to find a creative voice to express the beauty, pain and duality in your life.
- Too much Piscean influence can cause you to drift and miss opportunities through aimlessness.
- Piscean film director David Putnam expressed this sign's sentiment: 'Film is an art form of uniting in peace that family of man of which we are all part.'
- Pisces rules the feet, and its motto is 'I redeem'.

The houses

The last main factor in the birth chart is the houses. Just as there are 12 signs, there are 12 astrological houses that closely reflect these. The houses are subdivisions of the Earth's rotation on its axis during a day.

   The word 'house' suggests a place where one resides, and this is exactly what happens in a birth chart: the planets occupy different compartments of the chart, showing the area where their energies will 'be at home' and function best.

   The houses of the birth chart are numbered in sequence from the first to the twelfth house. The meanings of the houses have a close affinity with the 12 signs, e.g. Aries as the first sign places great value on self-motivation, and the first house is to do with the self meeting the outside world. Before you find out where the houses are in your chart you should look at your ascendant.

The ascendant

Astrologers use very specific calculations to 'cast' the horoscope or birth chart for a specific time and place of birth. This is why astrologers want to know the exact time of birth. The moment of birth determines the degree of the zodiac rising over the Eastern horizon – the 'sunrise' point – also called the ascendant. This is the point at which the unique personality comes into being.

Your ascendant represents your individual view of the world and gives you your sense of identity: your physical appearance, the typical way you respond to things, your unique mind-set. The ascendant is the beginning point of the first house, the house of the self.

- If you can access the internet, the simplest and quickest way to calculate your ascendant and birth chart is to visit the Swiss Astrodienst site at www.astro.ch which has a free on-line chart calculation service.

What do the 12 houses represent?

- **First House**: self-awareness and self-image, personal style
- **Second House**: personal resources, earning power
- **Third House**: thinking, learning and communicating
- **Fourth House**: home origins, our family roots and traditions
- **Fifth House**: Playing, loving, children and love affairs
- **Sixth House**: health, service, employment
- **Seventh House**: relationships, co-operation, marriage
- **Eighth House**: sex, psychological change, regeneration
- **Ninth House**: education, philosophy, religion, travel
- **Tenth House**: vocational aspirations, career, public life
- **Eleventh House**: ideals, social values, friendship
- **Twelfth House**: mysticism, spirituality, solitude

Putting It All Together

Interpreting the birth chart

The birth chart is designed to present a complete picture of a whole human being. An astrologer's analysis of a chart will never be a definitive statement, but it will be an exploration of a many-sided image. This is a two-way process involving the astrologer and the client.

In fact, when learning how to understand a birth chart, the best and most relevant information will come from its owner. For example, if you have a chart in front of you with Moon opposing Uranus, you will start with basic principles:

- Moon relates to feeling, imagination, belonging, safety
- Uranus relates to sudden change, freedom, originality.

Together the two principles could mean many things, such as :
- a highly original imagination
- or a person whose mother was unusual
- or a freedom-loving personality
- or a dislike of emotional commitment

But what does it mean for this person? Here is where describing the principles and then getting some feedback from the owner of the chart will teach you astrology! And the best way to learn is to practise with friends and family. If you decide to study astrology for yourself, then it can become a tool for personal growth and solo exploration. Insights that come from chart analysis can help to unlock thorny personal issues, and the beginner in astrology should always remember that seemingly 'difficult' parts of the chart will eventually give depth, endurance and positive potential to the character.

An astrologer will always use intuition as much as intellect in their interpretation of a birth chart. After carefully setting up the chart and studying its structure and its features one by one and the way they all relate to each other, the astrologer will pause in order to allow their intuitive imagination to go to work.

Forecasting future trends

Astrology can be used to analyse the potential of future times in general, and more specifically for individuals, countries and companies. It is understandable that many people feel a sense of awe and terror about the predictive aspect of astrology, but some phases of our lives demand more courage and strength than others, and astrology can help us to identify the timing of these phases and the meaning they may have for us.

Forecasting versus predicting

No matter what methods of forecasting are used, always remember that astrologers can only identify trends and processes; they cannot see 'events' as such. Just as a wise sailor works with the wind, tides and currents, so astrology provides a map of the prevailing climate. Given the awareness that astrology can provide, we all have the free will to work more consciously with the energies of the time and turn them, through our own choices, towards the best and most true our lives can be.

Resource Guide

The annual yearbook *Astrology* is an invaluable resource guide that promotes astrology throughout the world. It is available directly from the address below. Please contact the trust for current prices

The Urania Trust
BCM Urania
London WC1N 3XX
Tel: 020 7700 0639
Fax: 020 7700 6479
www.urania.org.

The other major resource guide for news and information worldwide is available from:

The Astrological Association of Great Britain
Unit 168, Lee Valley Technopark
Tottenham Hale
London N17 9LN
Tel: 020 8880 4848
Fax: 020 8880 4849
If you want to study yourself contact:

The Faculty of Astrological Studies
54 High Street
Orpington
Kent BR6 0JQ
Tel: 07000 790143
Fax: 01689 603537

The Mayo School of Astrology

(Principal: Jackie Hudson, D.M.S. Astrol.)

Alvana Gardens

Tregavethan

Truro

Cornwall TR4 9EN

Tel: 01872 560048

email: jackie.h@virgin.net

The Centre for Psychological Astrology

BCM Box 1815

London WC1N 3XX

Tel/Fax: 020 8749 2330

email: cpalondon@aol.com

If you want to look for a practitioner who has undergone formal training with an organized school, The Association of Professional Astrologers (APA) publishes a list of its members. Write to: The Secretary, 80 High Street, Wargrave, Berkshire RG10 8DE.

If in the US, contact the NCGR, PO Box 38866, Los Angeles, CA 90038, tel: 818 761 6433.

Personal recommendation is always a good way to find an astrologer.

The Astrology Shop, 78 Neal Street, London WC2H 9PA, Tel: 020 7497 1001, offers computer-generated reports which range from birth chart analysis, to chart comparisons and reports on your current and future trends.

A wide range of computer programs can produce professional reports for natal charts, chart comparisons and for forecasting. A list of such software can be found in the Astrology Yearbook and on the urania web site. A few of the most important suppliers can be contacted at:

- www.world-of-wisdom.com
- www.electric-ephemeris.com
- Janus: Tel/Fax: +64–9–373–5304
- Matrix: www.astral.demon.co.uk or
- thenewage.com
- Solar Fire: roy-gillett@dial.pipex.com
- Esoteric Technologies Pty Ltd, Tel/Fax: +61–8–331–3057
- Free Ware can be accessed through astrology-world.com under 'Freebies'.

Astrology can be found on the Net at:
www.urania.org
www.astrologer.com
astrology-world.com
www.astro.ch